T0368498

The
Unsinkable Col. Chambers
Misadventures on the Low Seas
Illustrations and Epigrams
Laugh While Learning Life's Lessons

By

John H.W. Rhein III

John H.W. Rhein III

P.O. Box 313 Saunderstown RI, 02874

A Green Rhino Pixelbook

To order additional copies of this book, contact:
Xlibris
844-714-8691
www.Xlibris.com
Orders@Xlibris.com

ISBN: Softcover   978-1-6641-9860-9
         EBook   978-1-6641-9859-3

Print information available on the last page

Rev. date: 02/01/2022

Introduction

The Unsinkable Col. Chambers

Since 1957, Col. Chambers has been a part of my life. He was the by-product of a futile search for a companion for a delightful little print my wife, Phyllis had picked out titled, "Mr. Sponge Arrives at Sir 'Arry's." by 19th century cartoonist, John Leech. After some discussion, it was clear the picture was too small to make a solo statement, but our search for a companion or two lead to frustration. Happily our dismay had a flip side: It sparked my creative engine, and so, Col. Chambers was conceived as a "do it yourself art project."

To re-create the feeling of our little Leech illustration my Col. Chambers episodes needed to be saturated with an aura of Victoriana, and, for humor, drenched in incongruity. These parametric challenges have lead to my sustained pleasure over the years as I sought out silly situations in which to involve my Col. . And surely my cup ran over when I found thinking up applicable epigrams to be a thoroughly enjoyable adjunctive treat.

Eventually, running out of places to hang originals, I began to give the pictures away to family members and close friends. When they were received with grateful chuckles, I was encouraged to publish some of the prints in a book. Voilà "Who is Col. Chambers?," my first downloadable pixelbook (heavy on illustration, shy on text). It was first published in a loose leaf notebook and then a wire bound version before being available in soft cover and an Apple App. It was followed by "Col. Chambers and The Walking Culture," and next "Horseing Around With Col. Chambers" (Not wishing to give readers the wrong idea about the Col.'s behavior, I deliberately mis-spelled the word Horsing), and now, to add to the series, we have "The Unsinkable Col. Chambers."

"The Unsinkable Col. Chambers" immerses readers in the "sailing culture" via a small hamlet on the banks of Rhode Island's Narragansett Bay, Saunderstown. A yacht club now exists where once there was a ferry to take passengers over to Jamestown where they could take another ferry to Newport. The Rhein's consider Saunderstown "family" country. We can't walk down our Willett Road without meeting a cousin or two. Everybody has a wave and/or a friendly smile, and some of the residents I've known all of my life.

The book will introduce readers to one of the traditions of the yacht club which could well have been conceived with the Col. in mind. Each year (with rare exception) the "Oceanology Award" is given to some deserving member who has exhibited the most conspicuous breech of good seamanship, and I am boundlessly grateful to a former yacht club commodore, Mike Pilson for letting me have the roster of award winners and occurrences for use in this book. It is to be noted the Col. is cast in the central character role for each aquatic atrocity used, and I apologized to him for making him the scape goat. Dear readers, it should be comforting to know, he couldn't are less.

Art work of eighteen hundreds often invited viewers to compose imaginary stories using the facial expressions and surroundings of a variety of subjects as prompts. I suppose it was a forerunner of today's cross word puzzling and was considered brain food. Since my pixel books are pledged to be long on illustration and short on text this venue is perfect for the Col. Chambers series. As you read on you'll realize I have exploited this "picture is worth 1000 words" phenomenon to the hilt, and where ever possible I have demonstrated the epigram "Less said, best said" with considerable agility. I think you will enjoy this romp with the Col. Its a quick read with an allegorical twist: you might be well advised to know FROG is and acronym for Fully Rely On God (and the Col. absolutely does) and horses are known to possess senses that are far superior to humans (horse sense is intuition power).

Have a great sail.

Col. Chambers Finds Himself on the Shores of Narragansett Bay

The Unsinkable Col. Chambers

Misadventures on the Low Seas

Illustrations and Epigrams

Contents

Introduction 1

Getting puffed up on public exposure is vainglorious. 7

Overreaching can be a trying exercise 8

You can never have too many friends. Cultivate them. 9

Better too early than too late. 10

Never let your start be your finish. 11

If there is no more room – something has to give. 12

Always have the right equipment handy. 13

Clear all impediments before proceeding. 14

Always make sure you are in the right class. 15

Red Right Returning – Always obey the rules. 16

Never be a drag. 17

Turtling means different things to different people. 18

Patience is a virtue. 19

Consider the " domino effect" before acting. 20

"Never give up- Never, never, never give up." 21

"When you take a licking keep on ticking." 22

Do as you would be done by. 23

Starboard tack (right) has the right - of - way. 24

Never be the cause of a negative effect. 25

Choose your skipper wisely. 26

Never overlook the power of suggestion 27

Tie up all loose ends. 28

It's likely snoozers will be losers. 29

Never pull the curtain until the act is finished. 30

Crawlers can be stallers. 31

Only dream the impossible. 32

Make sure your good intentions are accurately directed. 33

When you sink your boat keep afloat. 34

Look-out for potential snags. 35

Sailors should know how and where to reach. 36

Just when things are going fine - make sure you're holding the right line. 37

Good stories end with a punch line. 38

Epilogue 39

Dedication

Print collectors *Collector's editions

This book is dedicated with gratitude to those who have encouraged the continuance of the Col.

Chambers chronicles by looking at his books, illustrations, covers, cards, App, CD and prints, and/

or attending his book signings, talks, art exhibits, or visiting GreenRhinoPixelbooks.com, or who

are friends, mentors or members of supportive families. Please excuse any inadvertent omissions :

Brett **Adams**; Joanne & Ken #, Sydney **Adams**; Judy & Ed **Alzner**; Ed **Ambrosino**; Jean **Andersen**; Betty # (selected Col. illustration for Dutch Island Lighthouse brochure), Doris **Aschman** (when Commodore selected Col. Chambers for the cover of Yacht Club year book); Bob **Baer**; Ann & Norm **Baker**; Bruce **Balding** #; Jeanne **Benjamin**; Linda & Park **Benjamin**; Laura & Tony **Barboza**; Hannah & Basel **Barchuck**; Nancy & Bob, Courtney, Emma, Patrick **Basel**; Ernestine & Jack **Bash**, Louise **Barry** #; Eric **Benson** (first 2 volume order); Barbara **Bernard** (prize winner); O. John, Jr.*#, O. John III # & Anna #*, Otto J. IV & Billie #, O.J. V, Sunny, Joephine, Bob #, Rob, Lizzie, Alex & Rebecca #*, Emily, Abigail, Anna, Bill # & Sally, Oliver, Pearl **Betz**; Barbara **Beuerlein**; Adria & Charlie, Charley, Kate **Biddle**; Mary & Buckey, Buffie; John & Jill; Anne, & Will; John & Jen, Jack; Compton & Emile, Compton Jr., Finley, Charlotte; Katie & Peyton **Biddle**; Stephanie **Bird**; Betsy & Bob **Birchenough**; Stephanie & John , John IV, Madelin **Bishara**; Betty, Avery & Rolin, Tilden, Sam; Melissa, Perot, Ulie, Helen, Perot 3rd **Bissell**; Chuck **Bolduc** #; MJ & Gene **Bolter**; Bill **Bonadies**; Jean **Bowerman**; Seth **Bowerman** ; Martha & Ansel, Janet & Peter, Tim, Tina, Scott **Braseth**; Warren **Brown**; Craig **Brustad**; Paul **Bruehl**; Mary & Cal #, Alice, Beverly #, Charles, Robert **Buchanan**;; Jean **Cahill**; Dixie & Bob **Chapman**; Vito **Caporusso**; Colleen & David **Callaghan**; Jen Breslin; Mary Jane **Caldwell** (Garden City Historical Society exhibit curator); Bernie & Charlie **Cariello**; Sybil **Carton**; Virginia **Cauley** #; Helen & Sam **Cavior**; Nancy **Cerbus**; Virginia & Dick **Cheney**; Jane **Chute**; Melissa & Quent; Quentin, Cameron, Benjamin **Chafee**; Margaret & Bill, Spencer **Coffee**; Carol **Cook**; Dan **Coghlin**; Elizabeth & Jeremy, Sam **Collie**; Beth & Terry # (multiple volume gift packages); Bayard* # & Anne **Collins** (Collectors); Brent **Cliveden**# (tech guidance & inspiration); Brenda & Tony **Crawford**; Essie **Cruickshank**; Ryan Conan; Les **Cuneo***#; Ann & Mario **Cuneo**; Anne & "Mack" **Crisfield** * #; Stephanie **Cullum**; Empie & Dan, Katherine & Jamie, Sophie, Amanda, Christopher & Pam **Davis**; King **Davis**; Sandy & Nelson **DeMille**; Gloria **Denby** #; Suzanne **Dillenbeck** #; Bob **Dilensschneider**; Janet & Ward **Doerschuck**; Suzanne **Dowling**; Caroline **DuBois**; Sue Don & Nick (associate publisher GreenRhinoPixelbooks.com) **Dubowski** # *; Nancy **Dunnan** #; Harry **Dunning**; Natalie & Jacques **DuJoux**; Beezy **duPont**; Leah & Tom **Dryden**; Phyllis **Duntze**; Anthony **Durante MD**; Robert **Edelman MD** *#; GiGi & John **Edwards**; George **Ehrhardt**; Sandy & George **Engelke**; Josh & Rick **Evans** Roberta **Evers**;

Sandy **Fajans**; Marty **Farber** *; Chu Chu **Farley** *; Ellie (Willett Free Library book signing and illustration for Dutch Island Light brochure approval) # & Bruce **Ferguson**; Ann **Ferante**; Victor **Gallo** MD; Adrian & Bob,Taylor **Gang**; Gregory **Fayzakov**; Ros & Leslie **Fitzpatrick** #; Bob **Flaherty**; P.A **Freeman** *; Steve, Kip, Tim, Robert, Wally **Forbes**; Sheila **Foreman**; Ginny **Fortney**; Justin & Leigh; Carter **Frackelton**; Bessie & David **Fuchs** # *; Meghan & John **Fulweiler**; Barbara & Peter **Gall** #; Ellen **Gamber** #; Wendy & Steve, Toby **Gebb**; Bee & Curt **Givan**; Edith & Roger **Gerber**; Marie **Gillespie**; Anne & Larry **Glenn**; Ann **Gramstorff**; Sue & Mark, Joshua, Ben, Sam **Greenfield**; Jane **Greenleaf** # (home on cover art- bulk order patron); Vincent **Guido**; Stephanie **Dutkiewitz** & Hadley **Hadley**; Dianne **Hainsworth**; Sue **Hammen-Winn**; Lynne **Hale** #; Muriel & Doug **Hard**; Kris (prize winner) & Frank **Harder** #; Sue, Paul **Hazlett**; Billie **Hazzard**; Nancy **Hickey**; Matt **Hill**; Diana & John* **Herzog**; Jesica **Hagen** & Whit **Hill**; Jean & Bob **Henning**; Al **Hildebrand**; Alice **Hollett**; Elizabeth **Holman**; Martha & Walter **Hough**; B.A. **Howard**; Jane **Hughes**; Shirley **Jackson**; Jonathan **Janikies**; Cynthia **Jay***; Jo **Jenks**; Maureen & Thor, Honore, Hope **Johnson**; Margie **Johnston***; Lawrence **Jones***; Peter **Kai**; Nancy & Jack **Kane**; Dianne & Bill **Keegan**; Paula & Darren **Kiley**; Al **Kingon**; Trice **Kilroy**; Regina & Warren **Kraft**; Mary & Bob **Krenner**; Dottie & Lou **Kreyer**; Betsy & John **Lane**; Lois **Learned**; Michelle **Leavitt**; Ann & Frank **Lennox**; ; Sistie & Tom; Jimmie, Bill, Caroline, Nancy **Lewis**; Erminia & Eddie **Mack**; Lulu & Bob **MacDonald** *; Anthony **Massimillo** MD #; Jane **MacIntyre**; Ann & Vincent # *; Annie & Bill, Susan, Ann Carol **Madonia**; Jan **Mahood**; Peter **Marcionetti**; Ann Brooke **Mason** *; Kingsley **Mathew**; Jorg **Mayen**; Bev & Al **Maybach**; Arlene **Moore**; Sue & Rick **Moore**; Doug **Morrison**; Fran & Skip **Mays**; Louis **Marx***; John **McDermott**; Sue **McFarlane**; Jean **McMillan**; Sue & Dick **Mendes** (first advance order); Beth & Jim, Conor, Kevin and Chris **Mercadante**; Fred **Meyer**; Tony **Meyer**; Elizabeth & Bob **Metz** *; Richard **Miller**; Ed **Molenhoff**; Anne **Moffitt**; Maureen **Monk**; Sue & Rick **Moore**; Sarah & Charles **Morgan**; John **Munkenbeck**; Alice **Nalle** #; Lilyan & Van **Muran**; Hawsie **Nash**; Barbara & Ed **Nicholson**; Betsy & Jim **Nunnemaker**; Ashley & Cameron, Emma **O'Connor**; Clare **O'Connell**; Sheila **O'Connell**; Jill & Audie **Osgood**; Ann **Parkinson**; Joan & Mike **Pilson**; Susie & RB **Peelle**; Emily & Franklin (advisor) **Perrell** #*; Ellie & John **Perkins**; Joyce **Phelan** #*; Marie-Claire, Millicent **Pittis**; Rhoma & Howard **Phillips**; Jean **Plunket**; Anthony **Prisco**; Denny & Bill **Pugsley**; Barbel **Polanski**; Mary Jane & Tom **Poole**; Kathy & Tom **Powderly**; Doris & Denis **Quintillian**; Nina **Randall**; Posey **Randall**; Betsy **Ray**; Peggy **Renfrew** #; Robin **Johanson** & Chris **Kincade**; John **Knaus**; Skip **Laisure**; Jane Foster **Rhein** # *(first order), Jane Jr. #*, Peter # *(first bulk order), Phyllis Betz Rhein (long suffering wife of author who started it all) #, Petra **Kettler** & John IV **Rhein***#; Jen **Riley** (Willett Free Library Hostess); Agnes **Rimmels**; Rev. Ann **Ritchie** (Sunday School pupil); Mike - David*, Hannah **Roberts**; Maud **Robertson**; Julian*- Alex, Sarah & Spencer # Hollis , Hart, Josie, Whit **Robertson**; Liz **Roosevelt**; Sarane **Ross** # (first print purchaser); Karl **Rueck**; Cynthia & Pete **Sandford**; Jacqueline **Sandler**; Patsy **Sands**; Kay & Masaki **Sato** (hostess at 2nd book signing at CW Post College); Jane **St.Coeur**; Cy & Tex **St. Clair**; Maura & Erik - Andrew, Nolan, Kyle **Sayre**; Loretta & Eddie **Scena**; Jude **Schanzer** (Librarian East Meadow- First exhibit); Gregg **Schnoor** (Host of first exhibit wine & cheese party presentation); G. Richard **Schieffelin** (close friend - wedding usher)*#; Arthur & Terrica **Sarracino**; Sally & Hank **Schreier**; Helmut **Schuler** (arranged for Rotary Club speech); Marsha **Seaman**; Jane & David **Sellery**; Connie & Ben **Semmes**; Mary K **Sine** & Bill **Coldiron**; Virginia **Chapin** & David **Scheff** MD*; Shirley & Irving # - Kendall & Twig, Terricia & Rob, Savana, , Amber Aidan, Drusie **Sheldon**; Joan **Shepard**; Caroline & Wes **Singer**; R. Robert (Crusher) **Simmons**; Lynn & Mike **Soupious**; Tricia Dalto **Schetino** - **The Stewart Fund in Memory of St. Mary's & St. Paul's**, Gail **Dipalma** (former president of Stewart Fund) Patty **Siler**; Robin **Squibb***#; Margaret & Tom **Stacey***#; Freda and Bob **Stark**; Deborah & John **Stevenson** *#; Joan and John, Beth and Tony, Ginny **Stikeman**; John & Aloe - Walter **Stokes**; Jeri **Sedlar** (Author "Don't Retire Rewire" participated in "Beyond the Covers" book presentation at C.W. Post Library); Barbara (Willett Free Library, evening with Col. Chambers arranger) & Konrad **Streuli** *#; Nancy **Rubin Stuart*** & Bill **Stetson*** (friends & author of "The Reluctant Spiritualist"); Roy **Sullivan** PHD# (Audiologist - Col. Chambers on his office wall) Lisa **Tenner**; Val & Warren **Titus***#; Jim **Tiberg***#; Lynn & Pat **Tone**; Pat & Bob **Turner***#; Wendy **Warburton**; Dora & Cris **Waters** (prize winner - Willett Free Library signing); Barney **Webster**, Kathy & Locke - Aaron, Taylor **Webster** *#; Paula & Richard **Weir** *; Ann & Bill **Wesp***; Alison **West***#; Ady & Blue - Hadley, Kai **Wheeler***; Rita & Gerry – Rhoads, Peggy, Rachel & Kent **Williams**; Rodney **Windham** #; Peter **Yaremo**, Cinda & Ted **Yaremo**; Shoya **Zichy (**Author "Color coding personalities books"- participated in "Beyond The Covers" book signing)

Many names cited his dedication have left us, and many pursuers have not been mentioned. The author/illustrator has listed only those he knows have had some association with his Col. or have played a part in his jolly career. He is grateful for the support he receives and hopes those listed will make it a habit to curl up and cheer up with all three of his books. The Col. was conceived to leave his audiences smiling or in stitches. After all, "He's America's Good Humor Man".

Col. Chambers admires his cover picture

Getting puffed up on public exposure is vainglorious.

Col. Chambers gets stretched

Overreaching can be a trying exercise

Col. Chambers misses the raft

You can never have too many friends. Cultivate them.

Col. Chambers blows it

Better too early than too late.

Col. Chambers gets a hot foot

Never let your start be your finish.

Col. Chambers loads up

If there is no more room – something has to give.

Col. Chambers prepares for anything

Always have the right equipment handy.

Col. Chambers ignores a cleated sheet

Clear all impediments before proceeding.

Col. Chambers gets overtaken

Always make sure you are in the right class.

Col. Chambers points the way.

Red Right Returning – Always obey the rules.

Col. Chambers catches a bow — wow

Never be a drag.

Col. Chambers turtles

Turtling means different things to different people.

Col. Chambers waits for some horse power

Patience is a virtue.

Col. Chambers fends off a landing

Consider the " domino effect" before acting.

Col. Chambers stays in the race

"Never give up- Never, never, never give up."

Winston Churchill

Col. Chambers takes a licking.

"When you take a licking keep on ticking."

Timex

Col. Chambers takes off

Do as you would be done by.

Col. Chambers displays his ignorance

Starboard tack (right) has the right - of - way.

Col. Chambers causes collateral damage

Never be the cause of a negative effect.

Cover art for 2013 SYC Yearbook

Col. Chambers sounding

Choose your skipper wisely.

Col. Chambers avoids a gooseneck jibe.

Never overlook the power of suggestion

Col. Chambers goes adrift

Tie up all loose ends.

Col. Chambers takes a nap

It's likely snoozers will be losers.

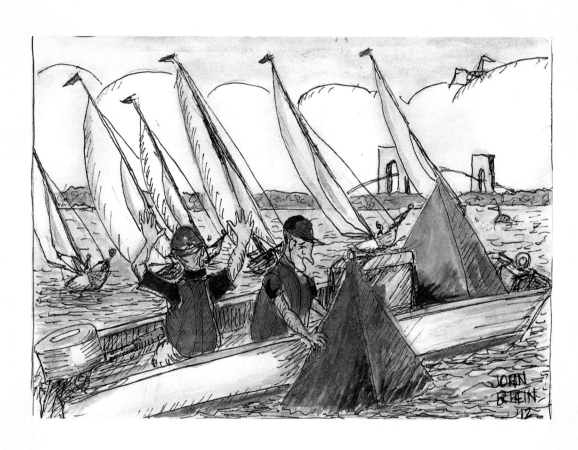

Col. Chambers prepares to lift a marker

Never pull the curtain until the act is finished.

Col. Chambers and company get in the way

Crawlers can be stallers.

Col. Chambers goes water skiing

Only dream the impossible.

Col. Chambers serenades the wrong ship

Make sure your good intentions are accurately directed

Col. Chambers abandons ship

When you sink your boat keep afloat.

Col. Chambers gets hooked

Look-out for potential snags.

Col. Chambers goes for the Oceanology Award

Sailors should know how and where to reach.

Col. Chambers holds the wrong line

**Just when things are going fine - make sure
you're holding the right line.**

Col. Chambers has some tea

Good stories end with a punch line.

Epilogue

It's a Laughing Matter

The Burning Question

Anyone who ever published a book would disagree with the title of this epilogue. Personally, I found publishing a book is far from being a laughing matter. Even before envisioning your book's presence, you must answer a simple question. In my case that was: *"what could anyone possibly get out of a book filled with funny colorful pictures with a parade of epigrams under them?"*

Curiously the answer to this first step came from a TV interview. One night, prior to composing "The Unsinkable Col. Chambers" I was sitting in my comfortable EZ chair channel surfing, when my attention was arrested by a conversation. The chat was between a well-known author, #Bill O'Reily and his contemporary, #Barbara Walters. She was about to launch her own talk show and Bill asked her, *"Who could possibly want to waste their time listening to small talk?"*

With no hesitation Barbara shot back a one-word reply, *"Everybody."*

She then went on to explain. *"Do you know anyone who doesn't enjoy a good laugh? Most people I know spend lots of time and treasure just to be entertained- right?"*

Train Your Brain

For me, imagining an audience of such size was inspirational, however, the heavy lifting came from putting together a book that would be both entertaining as well as instructional. It would have to be appealing to an ageless audience and do two things simultaneously. Could this be accomplished by scientific research? It's a matter of focus and interactivity. Readers should be entertained while they are subliminally exercising their brains and having fun. It must have the same appeal as a puzzle. Col. Chambers fans are encouraged to be interactive.

This thought train led to naming the characters in each picture, giving them some purpose for being there. The book must engage its readers challenging them to discover some of the humorous details in each artistically rendered episode.

Research Findings

Researchers have discovered those who laugh have sharper brains, fuller lives, and even better bodies. These obvious clues led to my revisiting my large assortment of Col. Chambers illustrations to find amusing or amazing episodes. That was easy: The Col. lives in a world of absurdity, frequently accompanied by animals. Even in "The Unsinkable Col. Chambers" where there is little or no shrubbery in which to hide silhouettes and line sketches the challenge is to find a frog or two (Fully Rely On God), a dog (Man's best friend) or a horse (For "Horse Sense) in each of the illustrations.

The Biddle Girls

I was given a treat last summer. Daughter Susan and I visited our cousins Ann and Will Biddle at camp "Hasanoanda" their Adirondack retreat. There, visiting at the same time were Compton Biddle and his three children. As one of their gifts, I gave the two Biddle girls a book containing dozens of Col. Chambers illustrations to pore through. To my delight both girls made their perusal a game of "Where's Waldo?" Who can find the most frogs, dogs, or horses if there are any? The present was a sensation, and the girls were a natural sounding board for the efficacy of my intention. As page after page offered a new reason to explore, those wonderful sounds of whoops and laughter filled the room.

The Catalist

There are seemingly endless numbers of activities in which the Col. has been involved, so as more and more are getting acquainted with him there should be lots of excited laughs and competitive outcries of "I Win" in the offing. Maybe Barbara Walters was prescient. Let's hope so.

Be kind to your brain with all three of his books. Col. Chambers was conceived to leave his audiences having fun or even laughing out loud.

He's America's Good Humor Man.

Printed in the United States
by Baker & Taylor Publisher Services